MIDDLE SCHOOL:
the real deal

MIDDLE SCHOOL:
the real deal

Juliana Farrell   Beth Mayall

From Cafeteria Food to Combination Locks

🏠 HarperTrophy®
An Imprint of HarperCollins*Publishers*

Middle School: The Real Deal

Printed in the United States of America.

For information address
HarperCollins Children's Books, a division of
HarperCollins Publishers, 1350 Avenue of the Americas,
New York, NY 10019.

Produced by 17th Street Productions,
an Alloy Online, Inc. company
33 West 17th Street, New York, NY 10011

Library of Congress Cataloging-in-Publication Data
Farrell, Juliana.
Middle school, the real deal : cafeteria food to combination locks /
by Juliana Farrell and Beth Mayall.
p. cm.
ISBN 0-380-81313-0 (pbk.)
1. Middle school students—United States—Juvenile literature. 2. Middle
school students—United States—Conduct of life—Juvenile literature.
[1. Middle schools. 2. Schools.] I. Mayall, Beth. II. Title.

LA229 .M378 2001
373.18—dc21   00-066218

First Avon edition, 2001

Visit us on the World Wide Web!
www.harperteen.com

Table of Contents

Welcome ⬤ middle ♂ school!

You've probably seen them at the mall or at the school carnival, looking so laid-back and cool. They're older . . . they're more confident . . . you can't wait for the school year to start so you can finally be just like them. That's right. At long last you'll be a middle schooler!

Before you enter the hallowed halls of middle school, there's some stuff you should know. You may think, I've already survived years of teachers and homework, so what's the big deal? But take it from us, middle school is different from grade school. There are the obvious changes—no recess, lockers (with locks!), crazy-loud bells, classes that have you running all over the building. And there are the less obvious changes— teachers' expectations of you, your friendships, the way you deal with your parents, the way you see your- self.

It may sound a little scary. But don't worry. This book is here to help you sort it all out. Before you know it, you'll be walking those unfamiliar halls with ease and confidence.

So are you ready? Time to pack away that Pokémon lunch box and get going to middle school!

Chapter 1

Ready, Set,
GO!

It's completely natural to be nervous on the first day of middle school. You might even be thinking, It's the first day—I've got to impress everybody.

Here's some inside information: Everybody is worried about that.

Remember, your friends and classmates

are going to be just as confused and

anxious as you during that first week.

So try to relax. You'll get through

it—together. In the meantime this chap-

ter is packed with tips that'll help you

stand tall on that first day.

GETTING READY

for

day

one

What?
I Have to Wake Up Earlier?

It's a fact: Usually the middle school day starts earlier than the elementary school day. This may not sound like a big deal, but actually it can be kind of tough to adjust to—unless you do a little advance preparation.

If you're not a morning person, try getting used to the earlier hours before school starts. For the last two weeks of summer vacation, start setting your alarm for the time you'll need to drag yourself out of bed. And here's the hard part: Try, really try, to get out of bed when the alarm rings. Don't just hit the snooze button and roll over, mumbling to yourself, "It's not really a school day." You also may want to skip that late, late show and go to bed at an earlier hour. By the time your first day comes around, you'll be ready to face the morning.

Here's another tip that may sound dumb but is actually key: Make sure you know when school starts. You'll be amazed at how many kids show up late the first few days because they never bothered to check. Also, if you're going to be riding the district school bus, make sure you know what time it arrives at your stop. If you're walking to school, try to get there a little early so you can find your homeroom (or your first class if your school doesn't have a homeroom period).

What Am I
Going to Wear?

Here's one area where the girls may have it easier than the guys. They can chat away on the phone and figure out what to wear on The First Day. But we're here to give both girls and guys some wardrobe help. Check out these dressing dos and don'ts for day one:

Do go casual. The last thing you want is to show up in a fancy party dress or a coat and tie when everyone else is wearing shorts and tank tops.

Don't try to break the rules—at least not on the first day. Read the dress code. If it specifically says no shorts, don't wear shorts. There's nothing quite like getting called to the principal's office on your first day of school.

Do break in your new shoes beforehand. You don't want to be one of the many people limping home with blisters because you saved your new shoes for the first day. Give yourself at least a week to beat up those brand-spanking-new sneakers.

Don't wear clothes you've never worn before. Of course you want to look nice, but you may feel uncomfortable if you're wearing unfamiliar clothes. If you want to show up in new clothes, make sure you wear them at least once before the first day. But really, there's no hurry to break in that new shirt or skirt—you have a whole school year to show off your wardrobe.

Do get a haircut—but . . .

Don't wait till the morning of your first day to try out a new hairstyle. If you're going for a new look this year—and why not?—make sure you give it a test-drive for at least two weeks before school starts. It'll give you time to get comfortable with the look so you can walk into your new school with your head held high instead of checking the mirror every five seconds.

Do try to chat with a friend about what to wear on the first day.

Don't decide to wear identical outfits—you're in middle school now. Besides, you want to show people that you're an individual, right?

Do feel free to reinvent your image. If you wore jeans and a rugby shirt every day in elementary school but now you want to go Hawaiian, we say go for it! Middle school is a chance for you to start fresh. Just be sure you try out your new look beforehand, in private.

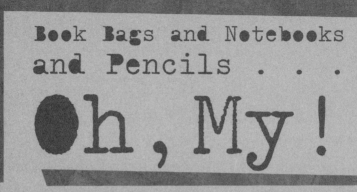

Book Bags and Notebooks and Pencils . . . Oh, My!

When you enter middle school, there are lots of decisions to make, and each one will feel like the most important in the world. Your school supplies are no exception.

What Should I Carry My Books In?

You're going to need some kind of bag since you'll be carrying books for several classes at once. Every school has its own trend as far as book bags or backpacks go, so if you want to go with the ruling style, you might want to wait until school starts to check out what's hot at your school. Then shop for one when you're buying any last-minute school supplies.

Comfort is key here, but it's also important to get a bag that has separate compartments for pens and pencils, your wallet, and other small stuff. You don't want to be constantly digging in the bottom of your bag for something to write with. Besides, that kind of disorganization can really get on your teachers' nerves.

Should I Buy One Big Binder or Lots of Little Spiral Notebooks?

With so many different classes to keep track of, what's your best bet when it comes to notebooks? Sometimes a teacher will tell you they prefer one over the other, but otherwise it's up to you. Check out this chart before you decide:

The Binder vs. Separate Spirals for Each Class

The Binder:

- You have notes for all of your classes with you at all times.

- A binder is big and bulky. Even if you have homework in only one class (yeah, right), you still have to bring the whole binder home.

- You can add more paper as you run out. Also, you can move pages around easily.

- If you lose your entire binder, you've also lost all your notes . . . for every class!

Separate Spirals:

- If you bring the wrong notebook to class by mistake, you won't have your notes in that particular subject available to you.

- Spirals are lightweight. And you can bring home only the ones you need.

- If you end up taking tons of notes in, say, English class, you may run out of paper and have to start a new notebook midyear. Once you start using multiple notebooks for the same class, things can get mighty confusing . . . and fast. Now, where did I put that notebook? Oh, and one other tip: A lot of teachers hate those scraggly edges that you get when you rip out sheets from your spiral. So if you do go the spiral route, make sure you buy the kind that have the perforations so you can tear off the scraggly edges.

- If you lose a spiral, at least you've still got the notes for the rest of your classes.

Another option: Bring one spiral (remember—perforated paper) or lightweight binder to all your classes and keep a set of folders—one for each of your classes—at home. At the end of the week put notes and papers for each class into their own labeled folders. This also offers a good opportunity to review the week's notes. But don't try this system unless you're a pretty organized person. It can get out of hand if you don't stay on top of it.

Let Me Just Check My Schedule...

Don't be shocked when you get a complicated-looking chart in the mail a week or two before school starts. This is your class schedule.

When you were in elementary school, you probably stayed with the same class full of students for the whole day. One of the biggest differences in middle school is that your classes and your teachers are more specialized. You'll probably have a separate teacher for each of your subjects. That means you'll see five to seven different teachers, classrooms, and groups of students every single day. Check out your schedule—you'll notice that each subject (math, social studies, etc.) is listed next to a specific time period, teacher, and room number. In most schools each subject lasts between forty and fifty minutes. Then the bell rings, and you'll have about five minutes to get to your next class or to the cafeteria for lunch. Chances are you're the only person in the entire school following that exact schedule. Pretty cool, huh?

When you first get your schedule, find out from your friends who's in which of your classes. It's always nice to see a familiar face in an unfamiliar setting. Maybe you can even find a friend to walk from class to class with.

Of course, it helps if you actually have a clue where your classrooms are. Most schools offer tours before school officially starts. If your school does this, it's a good idea to attend. If yours doesn't, ask if you can take a walk around the building before school opens.

schedule tip

School schedules aren't known for their artistic beauty. Make a cool copy of your own using a ruler, markers, stickers . . . whatever. Or if you're a computer whiz, design your own and print it out. Just be sure you copy all the information correctly!

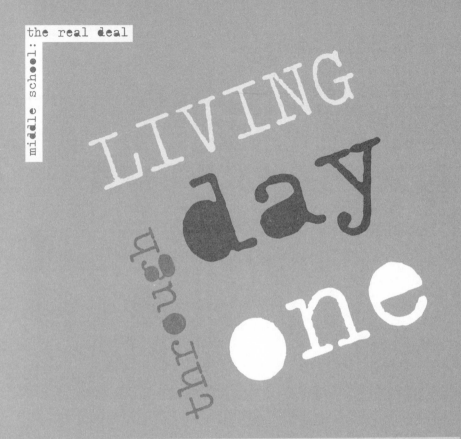

LIVING through day one

My Locker, My Home Away from Home . . .

In elementary school you probably kept your stuff in a cubby in your classroom. But most middle schools assign each student his or her own locker somewhere in the halls. (A few schools, especially very crowded ones, require that two or more students share a locker.) A locker is like having your own apartment—only much smaller. Each locker has either its own combination lock attached to the door or a latch where you can place a lock from home.

You should come prepared with a lock from home just in case the lockers at school don't have attached locks. And since you'll be keeping valuable stuff in there—books and personal items—you should be the only one who knows your locker combination.

Most students stop by their locker as soon as they get to school, then again before or after lunch, and again at the end of the day. As you get used to your schedule, you'll figure out the best times to stop by your locker. A word of advice: Don't leave food in your locker. It gets gross fast.

locker tips

- Make a miniature copy of your schedule to post on the inside of your locker door.

- Bring a few of your favorite pictures and posters and tape them inside the door. Better yet, how about some postcards or snapshots from your summer vacation?

- Lessen your chances of being locked out by thinking of a song you can sing the numbers to. Or write your combo on a scrap of paper and stick it in a zip pocket in your bag. (If your lock was supplied by the school, they'll keep a copy of the combo on file in the school office—so if you do forget it and you can't find that little slip of paper you wrote it on, you can always ask at the office.)

Home, Sweet Homeroom . . .

You'll notice that you have something on your schedule called homeroom. Warning: Just because it has home in the name, don't expect fresh-baked cookies and comfy sofas to curl up on.

Homeroom is a short period at the beginning of every school day. It's a mellow period where the teacher takes attendance and you listen to announcements (upcoming dances, new rules, whatever is going on that day), get notices from the principal, say the Pledge of Allegiance, and focus on getting organized for the day. In some schools homeroom may be tacked on to your first-period class, making that class a few minutes longer than others. Because it's not an academic class, this is one part of the day where you don't have to worry about grades.

Mail? For Me?

In the weeks leading up to your first day, your school will probably send you a student handbook. Take a step ahead by reading it—even if it makes you feel like a geek. Yes, it will probably be less than exciting, but you'll find out what happens if you're late to class three times . . . what happens on a snow day . . . the kind of valuable information you'll need to know. So spend fifteen minutes and review the material.

Class, Be Seated

Many teachers like to give their students seat assignments as a way of keeping track of them. Once you're assigned to a seat, you'll be expected to sit there for the whole year. Since you'll have a different seat in each class, it might get a little confusing. Jot down a note to yourself in the appropriate notebook, as in, Science: row by windows, third seat back.

Caution! Be Careful with Your Stuff

When you get a new CD Walkman or expensive video game, the first thing you'll probably want to do is bring it to school and show it off. Go ahead, but keep an eye on it. After all, a lot of other people would probably love to have it as well.

Keep your valuable stuff with you at all times. Don't bring it in on a day that you have to change for gym, and don't bring it to sports practice after school—gym locker rooms are one of the most popular places for theft. Don't even lock it in your regular locker. Somebody could break in if they know it's there. Locker theft is a lot more common than you might think.

What's That Ringing?

In most schools the bell rings at the beginning and end of every class period. When a class ends, you will have several minutes to get to your next classroom. If two of your classes are close together, you may even have time to run to your locker or maybe take a few minutes to chat with a friend. However, it's your responsibility to make it to the next class before the bell rings again.

You'll probably get lost at least once during your first day. If this happens, don't panic. Your best option is to ask a teacher—any teacher—where your classroom is. Why a teacher? Because other students may be just as lost as you, so they might end up steering you in the wrong direction. Also, don't worry about getting in trouble. Most teachers are pretty understanding the first few days of school. If you arrive at your class a couple of minutes after the bell rings, it's probably not the end of the world.

After that, though, you should make an effort to be on time. What happens if you don't make it to class before the bell rings? Maybe your locker won't open or an upset friend needs to talk. If you're late, your teacher will probably give you one or two warnings, but after that he or she will start to hand out punishments, like detention. Rules are rules, after all, and you should be sure to learn your school's rules . . . and punishments.

the social scene

For most people, one of the biggest deals about starting middle school is the idea that they'll have to make new friends. Think about it: You were with the same group of kids for years in elementary school. You knew everything about everyone. But now you're in a new place. Maybe you're going to a magnet school in a different district and you don't know anyone. Or maybe lots of your elementary school friends are here at middle school with you, but their schedules don't match yours. Or maybe you're even in the same classes as a lot of your friends—but you want to branch out and get to know a different set of people.

For whatever reason, the beginning of middle school is also likely to be a time for new beginnings with friends, too. And although we believe that in the long run, you'll be glad you made new friends, the first day of school can feel kind of lonely sometimes. Just remember, it's that way for everyone.

How Do Middle School Friendships Start?

They start the same way as your elementary school friendships. Don't think that just because you're in new surroundings, it'll be harder to make friends. Since you spend half your life there, school is probably the best—and easiest—place for you to make friends. All you have to do is reach out. It can be as easy as smiling at someone in your homeroom or saying hello to the kid whose locker is next to yours.

Good Conversation Starters

- Share common school experiences— "Did you hear that they're serving blood sausage for lunch today?"
- Give a genuine compliment—whether it's on their outfit or the goal they scored in gym, everybody likes to feel good.
- Ask about an interest you share. If the boy who sits next to you in homeroom plays soccer and you love to play, ask when team tryouts are or if he's ever seen a professional soccer game.

WHо dо I sit with at lunch?

If it turns out that none of your friends have the same lunch period as you, don't let it get you down. It would be nice to have a period of hang-out time every day, but you should also think of lunch as an opportunity to make new friends.

If you're flying solo for lunch, scout out your lunchtime possibilities in your first few classes. Let's say that in third-period math, you sit next to a girl who seems cool and friendly. Ask her what lunch period she has. If it turns out to be the same as yours, you could say, "Mind if I hang out at your lunch table today?" Then you can walk into the lunchroom with a destination already in mind.

It is possible that, especially on the first day, you'll have to eat lunch alone. Whatever happens, remember this: No matter how awkward you feel entering the lunchroom alone, you can be sure you're not the only one. Also, it's only one period. You can take anything for one period.

QUIZ: Do You Make Friends Easily?

1. You walk into the school cafeteria and all the tables are taken. Worse yet, all your friends have a different lunch period and you don't see a single familiar face in the crowd. You:

a) perch at the corner of a table full of strangers, inhale your lunch, and then hightail it out of there. You spend the rest of your lunch period hiding out in the hall with your nose buried in your math book.

b) stroll up to a table, take a seat, and introduce yourself around. Before you know it, you're all talking about your new classes and how cool it is to have your own locker. Better yet, everyone agrees to meet at the same table tomorrow!

c) take a seat at a table and offer to buy everyone lunch. Spaghetti and meatballs on me!

2. You stop at your locker in between classes and notice that the girl next to you has a picture of your favorite singer taped up in her locker. You:

a) whip out your fan club membership card and help her to fill out the enrollment form on the spot. So what if she's late for class? She'll thank you for it later.

b) ask her opinion about the latest CD and tell her about the big concert you went to over the summer.

c) don't say a word. Just because you like the same singer doesn't mean you have anything else in common.

3. Your social studies teacher asks everyone to introduce themselves on the first day of class. A boy in your row freezes mid-introduction and starts to stutter. The entire class breaks out in giggles. He is totally embarrassed. You:

a) panic. Oh, no. Now you know you're going to freeze, too!

b) have a laugh at his expense with everyone else, then when it comes to your turn, do a hilarious imitation of his stutter.

c) approach the poor kid after class and tell him not to sweat it. Everyone gets nervous now and then.

4. You're studying in the library when a fellow student approaches your table. He says, "Hey, you're in third-period gym, right? That was a great goal you scored." You:
a) graciously thank your gym mate and introduce yourself.
b) say, "Yeah, I know, wasn't that the most amazing thing you ever saw?" Then you launch into a play-by-play recap of the game.
c) mutter "thanks" but dive right back into your book.

5. You get appointed as a captain of a kickball team at lunch. Everyone lines up and you start to pick teams. You:
a) choose the best athletes in school and run circles around the opposing team.
b) only pick kids you know.
c) try to include everyone on your team—from the superathlete to the quietest kid in school.

Scoring
1. a) 1 pt. b) 2 pts. c) 3 pts. 2. a) 3 pts. b) 2 pts. c) 1 pt. 3. a) 1 pt. b) 3 pts. c) 2 pts. 4. a) 3 pts. b) 2 pts. c) 1 pt. 5. a) 2 pts. b) 1 pt. c) 3 pts.

If you scored 12 to 15 . . .
Over the top. Wow, you're the life of the party! But you might want to chill a little. It's possible that you're trying too hard to make an impression. You don't have to be everyone's pal. Remember, it's great to be friendly and outgoing, but there's a fine line between outgoing and overbearing.

If you scored 9 to 11 . . .
Right on track. If only everyone had as easy a time making friends as you do! You're doing a great job easing into a new school and striking a balance between keeping your old friends and starting new friendships. Keep on keeping on.

If you scored 5 to 8 . . .
In a shell. You might want to think about trying to come out of your shell more often. It's a hard thing to make friends, but it's even harder if you don't give yourself a chance. Even the smallest steps can make a big difference—a smile or just saying "hello" to someone can lead to the best of friendships. When it comes to making friends, you get what you put into it.

They Seem So Much
BIGGER
Than Me

As you walk to your first classes of the year, you may feel like those giant kids in the grades above you are staring down at you and laughing. News flash: Most likely, they're not. Especially during the first few days of school, the older kids will barely notice you. They'll be too focused on catching up with their friends and talking about their summer vacations.

Another thing to keep in mind is that at this time last year, the older kids were in your shoes. Sure, now they've made it through a year or so of middle school— they've already made new friends and adjusted to having more freedom. You'll see them looking cool and confident, and you might feel like you'd sell your soul to trade places with them.

But if you find yourself feeling intimidated or self-conscious in front of an upperclassman, stop and picture him or her as a kid in your grade, lost in the big halls and feeling small. Being new in middle school is a nerve-racking time for everybody. Everybody.

So that's it. You made it

through your first day. You figured

out what to wear, got your school sup-

plies, deciphered your schedule, found

your classes, and even survived

lunchtime. Congratulations! Now let's

take a closer look at your teachers

and classes.

teachers and CLASSES

In elementary school you spent the

entire year in one classroom, with one

main teacher. Now suddenly you're faced

with classes that are all over the map. On

top of that, you've got to deal with several

teachers, each with a different personality

and style of teaching. In this chapter you'll

find out what to expect from your new

classes and the people who teach them.

so many . . .

TEACHERS

Just like you're best friends with some people, you're going to really hit it off with a few of your teachers. Maybe they'll crack jokes and make class as much fun as possible, and you'll be disappointed when the bell rings at the end of the period. But there may also be teachers who you'll have a harder time relating to. You have to be prepared for teachers who may seem supertough at first or a little boring.

You probably won't love every one of your teachers, but luckily there will be a lot of variety. Use the chart on the next page to help you identify different types of teachers. We'll show you the most commonly found personalities and the pluses and minuses of each. Keep in mind, though, that most teachers are a combination of types.

Six Common Teacher Types

As you walk from class to class on the first day of school, see if you can identify your teachers among the general models below:

The Teacher Type	The Pluses
The best friend	He's like a stand-up comedian, making everybody giggle. You actually have fun when you learn, and you don't really mind doing homework for this class.
The rules-aholic	She has the same rules for everybody, so you never feel like she's picking favorites.
The "mom" or "dad"	Every comment somebody makes in class is "brilliant" or "right" or "excellent." With all this positive feedback, you'll be eager to participate in class.
The popular professor	Could she look any cooler? This is the teacher that half the class will have a crush on. She dresses in hip clothes and uses the occasional slang word. You would love to hang out with her on the weekend.
The lecturer	This teacher is so into lecturing that he won't notice you passing notes and chatting with your friends—or doing last night's homework for your next class.
The slacker teacher	She doesn't appear to like standing up in front of the class to teach, so she'll let you have a lot of "study time" and break you up into study groups often, which could help you get to know some new, cool people in your class.

The Minuses

ven your best friend has bad days—or a bad
veek. If you show up at this class expecting to be
ntertained and find this normally cool teacher in
crabby mood, you might take it personally.

his teacher will not accept homework unless
's done a certain way—say, in blue ink or on a
omputer. Also, being late for class might mean
etention, even if you were consoling a friend
vho didn't make the soccer team.

his type of teacher can be emotional, and he
ould be extremely disappointed in you if you
on't turn in your homework on time or if you
erform poorly on a test.

ometimes it seems like this teacher picks
avorites, which can make the left-out students feel
little jealous. Also, if the teacher appears to favor
articular students and you're not one of those
tudents, it may make you a little nervous about
pproaching her for help after class.

He also might not notice that 99.9 percent of the
lass doesn't have a clue what he's lecturing
bout. You may end up having to relearn all the
naterial—and wasting a lot of valuable study
ime—before a test.

t's easy to view this kind of class as a social
eriod instead of an actual class—but that kind of
hinking can come back to haunt you later on in
he year. Just because the teacher doesn't write
own every single word on the blackboard doesn't
nean she won't test you on the material.

Tips for Dealing

Just because you feel like this teacher's a friend,
don't think you can coast by without doing the
work. A teacher is a teacher, and all teachers
expect you to learn.

Never ask this teacher to bend the rules for
you. If she changes the rules for you, then everyone in the class will expect the same treatment.
The rules are designed for a reason—whether
to teach you discipline or to prepare you for,
gasp, high school—so follow instructions extra
closely and keep detailed notes when you write
down homework assignments.

If you're struggling in class or forget an
assignment, be sure to talk to the teacher
after class—it will show him that you really
care about your performance.

If you feel shy around her, remind yourself
that she's a teacher, not a movie star. Her reason for being there is to help you learn, so
don't be afraid to ask for more instruction.

Raise your hand and ask a lot of questions. If
you don't understand the answer your teacher
gives, raise your hand and ask again. Not only
does it help you understand the material, but it
shows him that you're really trying to learn,
which might make him reconsider his teaching
style a bit.

Try to use at least half of your in-class
study time to go over assigned reading.
And when you're in study groups, review
instead of chatting.

WHY DON'T MY TEACHERS
care
IF I FAIL?

They do care. In fact, most teachers want to help you any way they can. But one of the most important jobs of a middle school teacher is to teach his or her students independence and self-motivation. It's a key lesson to learn by the time you get to high school. In middle school, for the first time in your life, you and you alone are responsible for your grades. So is that scary or cool? Maybe a little of both.

Here are some rules to help you navigate your new independence.

Rule #1: Don't expect your teachers to tell you when you're not getting it.

In elementary school your teachers would check in regularly to make sure you were understanding each concept as they taught it. In middle school it's your job to monitor your own progress and to seek help when you need it. You're the only one who can figure out whether you really understand multiplying fractions. Don't wait until the test to find out for sure.

Rule #2: Learn each teacher's style.

Every teacher teaches differently—and you'll have five to seven teachers, whose varied styles you'll need to learn. How does each one point out important information that might appear on a test? Do they write it on the board? Do they distribute a handout? Do they simply suggest that you reread the chapter? Every teacher has a different method and a different set of clues, and it pays to learn them.

Rule #3: Ask questions.

If you don't get something, ask. You might feel dumb, but you know what? Chances are, there's at least one other kid in the class who has the same question you have—but doesn't ask because he or she doesn't want to seem dumb. So really, you're doing someone else a favor. Also, we think you'll discover that asking questions actually makes you feel smarter and more confident.

Rule #4: Talk in class.

No, we don't mean chat with your friends. We're talking about class participation—raising your hand and volunteering an answer in science or getting involved in a discussion about a short story in English. It's a talent that will serve you well for as long as you're in school. Speaking up in class only becomes more important in high school and college. In many classes your participation will be factored in your overall grade. It shows the teacher that you're interested and that you're making the effort to understand the material.

Rule #5: Don't head for the back row.

If you get to choose your own seat, pick one toward the front of the class. True, it may be harder to drift or socialize, but being front and center helps keep your attention focused on the teacher and the blackboard—where it should be. Where you sit may sound like a small thing, but it could make a big difference in your grade.

A word about these rules: Friends may tell you that only geeks sit in the front row or that it's not cool to ask questions in class. But they're as new to this independence stuff as you are, and they don't necessarily know any better than you. The important thing to remember is this: Independence doesn't just mean fewer rules. It also means you need to learn to listen to your own inner voice and figure out what's best for you. Which in the long run means that you need to start making your own rules—and sticking to them.

SO MANY subjects . . .

Suddenly in middle school you're going to be studying many more subjects than you've had before. Some students will have no trouble adjusting to the new program—but for others it may seem overwhelming at first. If you're worried, read the following descriptions of what to expect in each of your classes.

Language Arts

Depending on your school, you may have English, reading, and spelling and grammar as separate classes, but they'll eventually all be wrapped up into one class that's usually known as English.

What you'll learn: You'll really hone your reading and writing skills by doing a lot of both. You'll learn new vocabulary words, improve your grammar and spelling, beef up your reading comprehension, and even learn how to give speeches.

Why it's fun: First of all, you can dazzle family and friends with your expanded vocabulary. Second, if you like reading, you'll be happy to know you'll get to do so much of it! And as a bonus, you may get to act out plays in class as well as practice writing short stories and poetry.

Why it's challenging: You don't just read—you have to think critically about what you're reading and find themes and issues the writer was trying to explore. If you've never written an essay before, you will learn how to do it in this class. You'll find out how to present your ideas in organized paragraphs, starting with an introduction and finishing with a conclusion. Also, you will learn the idea of outlining and creating a "rough draft," which is a practice version of an essay before you turn in the final paper. You'll learn how to focus your ideas and how to express them clearly and correctly. And luckily you'll be given more than one draft to get it right.

Math

What you'll learn: Middle school math is likely to be more challenging than the arithmetic you tackled in elementary school. You'll learn all about square roots, exponents, and algebraic equations and maybe even some geometry. Also, there will be fractions at every turn. And don't forget the math you've learned up till now! You'll have to apply it as the building blocks for middle school mathematics.

Why it's fun: Think of math as a puzzle or game, where you need to put all the pieces together to come up with a solution. You'll learn basic logic and problem solving—skills that you will need to master when it's time to face high-school-level calculus and algebra.

Why it's challenging: Beyond elementary school, math isn't about counting things. You actually have to use your imagination to picture three-dimensional diagrams and shapes. Math requires you to memorize equations, which can take patience and a lot of study time. Getting good at math involves a great deal of repetition, no matter how smart you are. The more you practice, the better you'll fare come test-taking time.

Science

Love those TV specials on killer volcanoes and tornadoes? Always wondering what that constellation is? Earth science, some chemistry, and some biology will most likely be covered in middle school science classes. You'll learn the ins and outs of the natural world and the part that we—and you—play in its development.

What you'll learn: The basic scientific principles you learned in elementary school will be further explored—and put to the test—in middle school. And since modern science and technology is constantly changing, you'll discover groundbreaking ideas and theories that your parents didn't even know about when they were in middle school.

Why it's fun: Want to be a mad scientist? Well, in middle school you'll enter the wide world of experiments and laboratory tests. You'll get to observe tiny organisms under a microscope and spend time studying heat, light, electricity, and the environment.

Why it's challenging: Some scientific concepts are complicated and hard to understand. Also, you don't play a hundred percent of the time. You'll have to keep careful notes during your experiments. And one more thing—in some schools you have to dissect insects or other animals to learn about biology. That can be rough if you're at all squeamish.

Social Studies

Are you a master of memorization? Then you'll love social studies, which involves remembering all kinds of dates, names, and places. But are there any other bonuses to knowing this stuff? Of course! Social studies is essential to understanding the world we live in today. Every time you pick up a newspaper, you have the opportunity to learn not only about what's happening today but also about what happened years ago and where we may be heading in the future.

What you'll learn: You'll cover the history, past and present, of many world cultures, starting with your own. You'll probably get a social studies textbook, but in addition your teacher may assign you to read your local newspaper. As we said, you'll learn a lot of dates, names, and places, but you'll also study concepts like democracy and communism.

Why it's fun: Social studies involves a lot of imagination. You can place yourself in George Washington's boat as he crosses the Delaware River. Or how about at the Continental Congress at the signing of the Declaration of Independence? It's like going to the movies—in your head! Also, social studies teachers will often assign you cool projects, like cooking food from another culture.

Why it's challenging: You'll cover a little of everything, from ancient civilizations to the Industrial Revolution. It's fascinating stuff, but some people may find all the information a lot to remember. Also, you really have to be able to use your imagination to make some of the more alien civilizations come alive in your mind.

World Languages

Most schools will offer you the opportunity to choose what language you'd like to study. The most commonly found world languages on the middle school level include Spanish and French and occasionally Latin or German. The trick is picking one that appeals to you—because chances are this is the language you'll be studying through high school.

What you'll learn: Learning a new language not only allows you to speak with people from other countries but also gives you insight into cultures different from our own.

Why it's fun: You learn a new language—what isn't cool about that? If you're a world traveler, you'll be able to impress family and friends with your world language skills.

Why it's challenging: What comes naturally to you in English can be pretty tricky en español. Or en français. Check out the sidebar for more details on specific languages.

How Do I Know What Language to Pick?

Should you pick the same language as your friends? If you think your friends will study together or practice speaking together, it makes sense to be in the same class. But if you pick a language only because your friends are pressuring you—and you'd rather study something else—think again.

Or should you pick the language that seems the easiest? Well, maybe. Right now you probably have no idea whether languages will come easy to you. But just because the first year of a language is easy doesn't mean it'll be simple in year two . . . or year three! Besides, if you pick a language class only because it has an easygoing teacher, you could be in trouble in high school—the teacher there could be hard! Then you might just be stuck with a language you hate.

So the bottom line? Pick the one that sounds like the most fun to you or relates to your family and background.

The Real Deal on Languages

The lingo: French
The good: It's oh so romantic—very popular with the girls (useful if you're a guy).
The bad: Some people find the pronunciation very difficult.

The lingo: Spanish
The good: It's spoken in many parts of the United States. You'll find many opportunities to use it.
The bad: Because of rumors that it's the easiest language, the slackers may take over this class.

The lingo: Latin
The good: Believe it or not, Latin is one of the important contributors to our own language, English. There are lots of English words that come from Latin roots. It's cool to find out this stuff. Also, since Latin is the direct root of both French and Spanish, knowing Latin makes learning those other languages a breeze.
The bad: It's a dead language—meaning no one actually speaks it anymore—so it won't help you out if you're ever traveling abroad.

The lingo: German
The good: German comes from the same root language as English. Although they sound totally different when you hear them for the first time, actually you'd be amazed at how many German words are really very close to English words.
The bad: German has complicated grammar, with things called cases, which means you have to learn lots of different endings for each noun and adjective. It's considered a pretty difficult language to learn.

Physical Education

Also known as phys ed, PE, or gym. This is a class you'll probably have at least twice a week. It's an opportunity to learn a little about all the different sports out there. It's also a good time for stretching your muscles and blowing off steam—especially now that you don't have recess anymore.

What you'll learn: The exact sports you'll play will vary, depending on what kind of facilities your school has. Some of the sports you might do in PE are basketball, volleyball, soccer, gymnastics, field hockey, racket sports, flag football, wrestling, track and field, lacrosse, softball, dance, aerobics, weight training, and handball. You'll also probably take fitness tests and learn about how to exercise properly so that you don't injure yourself.

Why it's fun: Come on—what's not fun about whacking a ball around and being allowed to run and yell for forty-five minutes?

Why it's challenging: You might find there are some sports you're just not that good at. Also, you might feel self-conscious about how you look in your gym clothes. But don't worry too much about this—everyone feels self-conscious in their gym clothes. Your classmates are probably too busy worrying about how they look to check you out.

Electives

The word *elective* comes from the word *elect*—which means to select or make a choice. In this case, you'll probably have the opportunity to choose some of the courses you will be taking. (Some middle schools might choose for you—it depends on your school.)

What you'll learn: The most common electives are art and music. However, elective topics may range from TV production to wood shop to home economics to theater arts. The courses offered will depend on your specific school.

Why it's fun: You get to develop new talents hands-on and participate in activities with students who share your own common interests.

Why it's challenging: You'll find out what you're good at—maybe cooking or car repair? But you might also find a few things you aren't good at—and you'll still have to stick with them for an entire marking period.

Why Are My Friends in Different Classes?

When you were in elementary school, there were some subjects you were really great at, right? When the teacher assigned work in class, maybe you were always the first person done. And maybe there were other subjects that just didn't click with you. Sometimes it seemed like no matter how hard you studied, you were always the very last person in the class working on a test while everybody else was finished and chatting away. Sound familiar?

In middle school you may be grouped with students who learn at the same speed that you do. For example, if you zoom through your math problems at the speed of light, you'll be placed in the track 1 math class. If you're an average math student, you'll go to the midlevel track 2, and if you need a little extra help, you might be placed in a track 3 class. And this doesn't apply only to math—many of your classes will be divided up like this.

The track numbers don't mean anything—they don't appear on your report card or affect your grades. You shouldn't feel embarrassed if you're in a track 3 class, and you shouldn't feel like you're king of the world if you're in a track 1 class. Everybody has certain subjects they understand more quickly than others. Maybe you need extra math help but you write incredible short stories. Now that you're in a class with people who learn the way you do—and at the same pace—you might understand the "harder" subjects better because you might feel more comfortable asking questions.

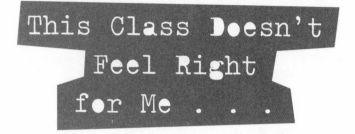

This Class Doesn't Feel Right for Me . . .

There's always a chance that one of your classes isn't a perfect match for your learning speed. For example, if you know the answer to every question the teacher asks or if you're completely lost about what's being discussed, you could be in the wrong track.

If you feel that this is the case, talk to your parents or your school counselor. However, before you make any big decisions, give yourself time to adapt to your new classes. If your friends are in other tracks, ask to see their assignments. Try to judge if you could keep up with the work or if it seems too hard or too easy for you.

If after a few weeks you don't feel any more comfortable and adjusted, talk to your parents about changing your schedule. But don't switch classes just because you want to be with your friends. You have a lot of school ahead of you, and making that mistake could have a serious impact on your grades and course selection down the road.

WHAT IF THERE'S
something I just
DON'T GET?

Here's a simple fact that everybody seems to forget: School is the place to learn things, not to show the teacher how much you already know. So when you are hopelessly lost in a class, you shouldn't hide your confusion. If you act like you know what's going on, you'll crash and burn on the next test. There are a few things you can do to avoid falling behind.

Bug your teacher. Most teachers are required to be in their classroom for at least a half-hour after school—that's a perfect time to go in for extra help. Let your teacher know that you'll be coming by after school. Be sure to go in with a list of stuff that's confusing you so the teacher doesn't have to guess what's wrong. Your teacher will realize that you're someone who takes the class seriously, which could help you out come grading time! And won't it be cool if . . . after a half-hour of one-on-one studying with the teacher, you're totally caught up?

Bug your parents. Why not? They had to learn all this stuff themselves, way back when. Just be sure that they help you—and that doesn't mean they do the work for you. If that happens, you'll be just as lost as before. Remember, your parents aren't the ones who will be tested on the material. And won't it be cool if . . . your mom is a brilliant physicist who practically invented the topic you're confused about in science? After a few sessions with your mom, your teacher might even be so blown away by your Einstein-like understanding that you can skip out on class for the rest of the year! (Just kidding!)

Bug your older siblings. Lucky you—your older sister took the same social studies class three years ago. She can be a big-time help. However, you won't be doing yourself any favors if you copy from her old notebooks. Ask her to go over confusing problems or assignments with you. Yeah, you may have to do her chores for a week, but at least you'll be getting better grades. And won't it be cool if . . . your older sister is a compulsive Web researcher and she actually helps you find out stuff about Japanese culture that isn't covered in class? Extra-credit points for you!

Bug a tutor. If you're having problems with more than one topic in a certain class, the best thing to do is to find a tutor who can help you at least once a week. Usually they're hired, so your parents will have to pay them. They may be either teachers from other school districts or older students. You can arrange to meet them either at your house or in the school library. And won't it be cool if . . . your tutor is so excellent that you actually become the master of that subject—and then you hire yourself out as a tutor?

Bug another student. You won't have to stay after school, and you won't have to pay them, which are both big bonuses. But sometimes other students are just as confused as you, so you could end up misunderstanding the topic even more than you did in the first place. So think about who you're asking for help. And won't it be cool if . . . your study buddy turns out to be a really cool person? You might just end up with a good new friend.

the new alphabet: A, B, C, D . . . F

Middle school is the time when teachers start using letters to grade students' performance. Here's a breakdown of what the letter grades mean:

A = outstanding student
B = good student
C = average student
D = below-average student
F = student does not pass the class

Each letter grade can also have a + or − sign after it. An A+ is the highest grade you can receive. A D− is the lowest grade you can get and still pass the class. If you get an F as your final grade in a class, you might have to repeat the class.

So what happens to the grades you earn in middle school? Well, in a few years high school guidance counselors will examine your grades and decide what level classes to place you in. Your middle school grades aren't a part of the record or transcript that you will need to get accepted into college, but they do affect what high school classes you'll be enrolled in. They can also affect your admission to high school if you apply to a private or parochial school or a magnet public school.

What's So Special About "Special Classes"?

You might notice that some students are in special programs that take place during regular class time. No—they aren't off playing video games or getting massages. They're probably in a special program, like one of the following:

Gifted and Talented Program

The gifted and talented program is an intense learning environment for students who are above average in certain subjects, like science or English. The program involves smaller classes that focus on group discussion. Being in this program doesn't mean you're better than everyone else—it just means that you have a better understanding of a specific subject.

Classified Program

Sure, it sounds like FBI training, but students in this program aren't hanging out on the *X-Files* set. Students in a classified program have learning disabilities. A common learning disability is dyslexia, a condition in which the brain has trouble processing written words. For example, a dyslexic student might confuse letters like *d* and *b* or might have a hard time recognizing seemingly simple words like *the* and *of*. But the same student might be a math whiz or do incredible oral reports in social studies.

If you're in a classified class or if you know someone who is, don't think that you or they are less intelligent than everyone else. These classes cover most of the same topics as the unclassified courses, but the information is taught in such a way that the classified student can better comprehend the material.

Famous People Who Were "Classified"

Some people believe that artistic creativity can actually be linked with certain kinds of learning disabilities. Although scientists don't yet know enough about how the brain works to say whether or not this is true, take a look at this list of famous artists who are believed to have been dyslexic. What do you think?

Leonardo da Vinci (painted the Mona Lisa)
Michelangelo (sculpted the famous statue of David)
Hans Christian Andersen (collected and wrote fairy tales)
Lewis Carroll (wrote Alice in Wonderland)
Mark Twain (wrote Huckleberry Finn)
Pablo Picasso (painted Guernica)

How Can I Catch Up After a Sick Day?

When you're sick at home, the last thing you want to think about is doing your homework. But if you don't try to stay up-to-date, you could fall behind big time. Part of being a middle schooler is being responsible for getting work done—catching up after a sick day is a smart way to prove you're a serious student!

How to stay in the loop? If you know you'll be staying home one day, call a friend or your study partner in the morning before school and ask them to get your assignments and any handouts from your classes. Maybe they can even drop off your work if the two of you live near each other. Just be sure to return the favor when your friend or study partner misses a day.

Homework Is a Full-Time Job

A big change you'll notice during your first week in middle school is that there is a lot more homework than you had in elementary school. However, with a little dedication on your part, it's manageable—and it's a good warm-up for high school, where you'll have even more homework! A sample night's homework might be . . .

September 27

Language arts: Read the short story on pages 52 through 59. Answer questions 1 through 3 on page 59. Outline of essay due on Oct. 4.

Social studies: Read about the burial practices of the ancient Egyptians in chapter 1. Answer questions 1 through 5 on page 32.

Math: Do questions 1 through 31 (odd) on page 40.

Science: Lab write-up due on Oct. 1.

French: Do all exercises on pages 23 and 24. Write in complete sentences.

Health: Answer questions on page 10 (human sexuality). Find a magazine or Internet article on puberty by Sept. 29.

How can you get it all done—and still have time for soccer practice and, oh yeah, relaxing? The first step is keeping track of it all, so it's a great idea to have one place where you write down all your homework assignments. You can buy a daily planner and use it to keep track of schoolwork as well as other activities like practice, baby-sitting, and parties. This way you can actually see when you have a free day to buckle down and get some serious work done.

Another good strategy is to invest in a mini-notebook especially for writing down assignments. That way all of your homework is on a single sheet, and you can also flip ahead to write in long-term assignments, like if you have an English essay due in two weeks. Keep the pad somewhere that's easy to get to, like the front pocket of your backpack.

As you get to know people in each of your classes, exchange phone numbers with a study partner in each class. Write their numbers on the inside cover of your homework notebook. This way you can call your study partner if you get home and realize you wrote down the wrong information.

A few rules for keeping it all under control . . .

Rule #1: If you're using a mini-notebook, put the date at the top of each page.

Rule #2: Make sure you copy the assignment correctly, including the name of the subject. That way you won't end up doing page 39 in math instead of page 39 in science!

Rule #3: Write down the specifics. If your teacher says to do three questions on a page and you wrote down only the page number, you might end up doing the wrong three questions.

Rule #4: Think about the order in which you tackle your assignments. If you're tired or you haven't eaten dinner yet, start with your strongest classes. Leave the more difficult ones until after dinner (or after a nap!), when you have more brainpower. If you're too busy to get it all done, do the homework for the classes where your grades are the worst—it'll keep you from falling farther behind. Note: Don't just do your homework in the order of your classes. You might find that your homework for your last class is always done poorly, when you're eager to get to bed!

Rule #5: Highlight or cross out each assignment as you finish it so you can see your progress.

Help—I Have a Major Assignment Due!

Instead of giving you assignments that you can wrap up in one night, many teachers will now give you assignments that will take a few days or even a few weeks to complete. It's part of teaching you valuable time management skills. Here's a heads up: Do not put off long-term assignments till the night before they're due. You probably will, anyway, but hey, we warned you.

Why not wait? Well, because there's a good reason the teacher gave you a long time to work on the assignment. A research report on carpenter ants or a three-page essay on O. Henry's "The Gift of the Magi" is not an assignment that can be slapped together in just a couple of hours. If you do it that way, your lack of effort will most likely be reflected in a low grade.

If a big assignment seems terrifying to you, divide it into a few smaller chunks. Four nights of mini-assignments are a lot easier to face than spending five hours on Sunday bulldozing through the whole thing. For example, if you have to write an essay on a short story, you might break it up like this:

Night 1: Read the story. Take notes on important or confusing passages. Time: one hour.

Night 2: Reread the story and focus on the confusing parts. Write an outline of the three or four important points you want to cover in your essay. Time: one hour.

Night 3: Write the essay. Time: two hours.

Night 4: Read what you wrote and make any changes you think are necessary. It's also a good idea to have a parent read it over to catch grammatical and spelling errors. Time: one hour.

One more very, very important thing: Don't forget to reward yourself for a job well done! If you finish your essay or project early, go ahead and watch an extra half hour of TV or spend a little more time on the phone with a friend. You've earned it!

QUIZ:
What's Your Study Style?

1. When your teacher assigns a group project in history class, your first thought is:

a) "Yippee! Studying with my friends makes it so much more fun."

b) "Oh, no. Now I'll have to bug everybody to get their work done."

c) "Hmmm—how can I be partnered with the smartest girl in class so I won't have to do any work?"

2. Rrrring! Okay, pop quiz: The second the bell rings at the beginning of class, where can you usually be found?

a) Sitting in my seat, chatting with somebody nearby.

b) At my desk, notebook open, pen in hand, ready to take notes.

c) Copying somebody's homework in the back of the room.

3. What's your day planner used for?

a) Writing down my homework assignments and keeping track of important social events.

b) Keeping a detailed list of all my assignments, which I highlight to prioritize. I also keep a running countdown of days until major assignments are due.

c) I usually use it as a pillow when I nap in class.

4. Most often, where do you do your homework?

a) In my bedroom or the kitchen at home.

b) Somewhere ultraquiet, without distractions—the library.

c) In class, while the teacher's taking attendance.

Scoring
Find the letter you selected most often, then read your scoring section below.

If you chose mostly A's . . .
 A for Attitude
You know that being a good student is all about balance. Hey, who cares if you're on the honor roll if you're stressed 24/7 and can't remember the last time you laughed with friends? The way you're working is a good balance of serious and studious. Just don't be afraid to buckle down and focus when it really counts, like on a final exam.

If you chose mostly B's . . .
B for Brains
You've got all the right moves when it comes to studying. Work habits like these will get you far in life! Except one teeny tiny problem: Do you make time to relax? Chilling out for an hour a day is just as important as getting it all done. Otherwise you'll burn out or become so stressed, you'll have trouble concentrating. Pencil some downtime into that day planner of yours!

If you chose mostly C's . . .
C for Character
Slacking off isn't going to get you very far in life. And although you pretend to be stress-free, we're betting that you do secretly stress out about not getting your studying done. To boost your study savvy, start small, like taking an hour of your free time each day to work on homework for your hardest classes. And start using that day planner as more than a Frisbee!

ell, that's the lowdown on teach-

ers and schoolwork. But believe it or not,

that's not all there is to middle school.

Next, get ready to think about what you're

going to do after school (besides home-

work, that is).

Chapter 3

extra-
curriculars

n elementary school you probably

went home after school and hung with

your friends, right? Well, now that you're

in middle school, you'll still hang with

your friends after school—but you'll stay

at school, and you'll be doing some kind

of organized thing together. This is what's

known as an extracurricular activity.

Extracurricular means in addition to (extra) your regular schoolwork (curriculum). Usually extracurricular activities refer to school clubs, groups, and athletic teams. An extracurricular can also be an activity you do outside of school, like working with a religious or community group.

why should I SIGN UP?

Getting involved in extracurricular activities can help to develop your talents—whether you're a good athlete or speaker or writer. More important, extracurriculars are lots of fun. Here's what's good about them:

You'll learn how to do things by actually doing them rather than reading about them or watching them on TV.

It's an easy way to make friends since you will have something you enjoy doing together.

When you're under tons of stress, after-school activities can help you blow off steam and stay sane.

If you're already good at a certain sport or hobby, you can help others learn—and develop solid leadership skills.

If you join a club for something you've never tried before, you'll have the opportunity to learn about it without worrying about grades or tests.

HOW I GET involved?

At the beginning of the school year, the school will probably hand out a list of all the sports, clubs, and activities that will be offered. Usually one teacher will be in charge of each activity—and that teacher will be referred to as the adviser. When you figure out what activity interests you, ask when tryouts or meetings are held. If you're nervous about going alone, convince a friend with a similar interest to tag along. But even if you don't have a friend to join with, don't let that stop you. You'll make friends soon enough.

WHAT KIND OF ACTIVITIES

are out there?

Here's a sneak peek at some of the most common after-school activities. Check out the list to see what interests you, then talk to your school's coach or adviser to get more information.

SPORTS

Athletics are probably the most popular after-school activity. But before you choose a sport, think about what kind of player you are. Do you prefer being part of a team, or would you rather compete by yourself? Do you like contact sports or ones that require high endurance? The answers to these questions will help you find the perfect sport for you.

Soccer

What to expect: You'll learn a lot about team playing, and you'll build up endurance for stop-and-go running all over the field. Since there is no position that's always in the spotlight, you can still excel at this game even if you don't like being the center of attention.

Basketball

What to expect: You'll develop strong hand-eye coordination. Like soccer, basketball is a sport that relies heavily on teamwork, so you'll have to focus on being aware of your teammates. Basketball is also cool because you can play indoors and out-doors, alone or with a few friends. All you need is a ball and a hoop!

Baseball/Softball

What to expect: You'll use fast, aggressive running to get on base and field balls. Remember, keep your eye on the ball! You definitely need to be a team player, but in these sports you also get your own moment to shine when you're up at bat or making a play in the field.

Cheerleading

What to expect: You'll need good vocal skills, a strong (and flexible) body, and a good sense of rhythm. If you're a risk taker, cheerleading might be for you. Some of those pyramids and jumps can be a little scary!

Football

What to expect: You need to be physically strong and in top condition. Many positions involve sprinting or catching and passing skills. Football gets lots of attention, especially in high school and college. If you're into participating in a high-profile sport, this one's for you.

Wrestling

What to expect: Wrestlers depend on upper-body and leg strength. This sport also requires a great deal of mental discipline. An unusual feature is that since wrestlers are divided into categories by weight, you'll never be matched up against somebody who's way bigger or smaller than you.

Track and Field

What to expect: This is pretty much a solo sport unless you're running on the relay team. As you might guess, track practice involves a lot of running—both sprinting and jogging long distances to build up your endurance. But track and field isn't just about running. The "and field" part refers to all the other activities that can be part of the sport—high jumping, broad jumping, throwing the shot put or javelin, pole vaulting, and more.

Tennis

What to expect: Tennis is another mainly solo sport. At most, you'll play with one other person, in a doubles match. Tennis requires strong hand-eye coordination and lots of endurance. Running around the court may look easy, but it's not! It also helps if you're someone who likes to be in the spotlight. Because when you're on that court alone, all eyes will definitely be on you!

Other popular sports include . . .

Swimming

Gymnastics

Lacrosse

Field hockey

Boy Sports vs. Girl Sports

Most schools have separate teams for girls and boys. What's more, some sports are traditionally played only by boys, like baseball, football, and wrestling. Other sports, like softball, field hockey, and cheerleading, are traditionally thought of as girls' sports. However, in the last few years more and more girls have been playing football—and more and more guys have been joining the cheering squad. So don't think your gender limits your choice of sport. It ain't necessarily so.

QUIZ:
Discover Your Sports Style

1. When I'm on a team, I don't feel nervous—I feel challenged.

Yes, that's me: go to 2
No, not me: go to 3

2. At a party, I talk to almost all the guests before it's over.
Yes, that's me: go to 4
No, not me: go to 5

3. I have a tight-knit group of between five and ten friends who do everything together.

Yes, that's me: go to 5
No, not me: go to 2

4. I don't usually get psyched out when people try to intimidate me.

Yes, that's me: go to "Go, Team!"
No, not me: go to 5

5. When other people depend on me to win, I tend to mess up.

Yes, that's me: go to "Fly Solo!"
No, not me: go to "Stick to the Small Squad!"

Go, Team!

You love being around tons of people with the same goal in mind: winning! Sports you'd enjoy: soccer, basketball, field hockey, volleyball, baseball/softball, football, ice hockey.

Stick to the Small Squad!

A massive team tends to distract you. You prefer a small group of focused people on whom you can really depend during a game. Why not try: swimming, gymnastics, cheerleading, martial arts, tennis.

Fly Solo!

Having people push you to win stresses you out. You prefer to challenge yourself, which is why you should stick to one-on-one sports like: wrestling, track and field, rock climbing, golf, horseback riding, skateboarding, in-line skating.

performing arts

Looking for a future as a movie star? Or do you see yourself as a famous musician? Learning the basics of performing in middle school drama or musical productions can help you reach your goal someday.

Theater

What to expect: Usually schools hold at least one dramatic performance a year. It's often a musical, which requires acting, singing, and dancing. Drama clubs are open to anybody who's willing to audition. In addition, there are a lot of jobs for people who aren't interested in performing—like costume designing, props, lighting, stage crew, and makeup.

Chorus

What to expect: You'll learn how to sing in harmony and read sheet music, and you'll perform in a concert several times a year. And as a bonus, if you have a standout voice, you could be chosen to sing a solo!

Band/orchestra

What to expect: You have to know how to play an instrument, of course. You may be expected to know how to read sheet music, too. And you'll need to practice your instrument a lot, both in and out of school. Besides the regular band or orchestra, some schools have a marching band, where you get to wear a uniform and perform in parades. In high school, band members might go on trips to competitions and travel with the football team. You can get your start in the middle school marching band!

Other Cool
Extracurriculars

Your school might have a lot of extracurriculars or just a handful. What's available varies greatly from school to school. Here's a laundry list of other common extracurricular activities.

Student Council

What to expect: This is a group of students who are elected by the rest of their classmates. The student council plans things like dances and fund-raisers for class trips. It's a great way to develop leadership skills and learn to voice your opinion. The student council is also the place where any student can go with a complaint or suggestion about school policy. For example, if you think the dress code is too strict or if you believe the school should install a hot tub in the gym, tell it to the student council! The council members take students' concerns to the principal and propose changes to the school policies in question. (But we don't think you should get your hopes up for that hot tub. . . .)

Yearbook

What to expect: Many schools print a book at the end of the year that includes every student's picture and memorable snapshots of events that took place throughout the year. Members of this organization take pictures and collect the written material (class lists, quotes, etc.) that goes into the yearbook. They also help distribute the books at the end of the year. The yearbook staff also decides how the book will be laid out, so it's a great activity for artistic-minded people.

School Newspaper

What to expect: Many schools print a newspaper several times a year to keep students informed. It's also a great way to give the student staff journalistic experience. Newspaper staff members get to interview people and write articles, or take photos, or edit other students' work. Like in yearbook, you'll learn about layout if you work on the newspaper. You'll also learn to meet deadlines, which is a really valuable skill for the rest of your life!

Language Clubs

What to expect: As the name implies, these are clubs for people who want to get together and practice speaking a foreign language. If your school offers French and Spanish in its world languages program, it might also have after-school clubs for these languages. Language clubs may also compete against other schools' clubs.

WHAT IF MY SCHOOL doesn't have an EXTRACURRICULAR activity for me?

If you have a passion for an activity that your school doesn't offer, don't worry—you can probably still find a group of other students who are interested in the same thing. If you ask, chances are your school will give you permission to start your own school club.

Also, you don't have to do your favorite activity at school. Let's say you love ice hockey, but your school doesn't have access to a rink, or you love baseball, but your school is in the city and doesn't have a playing field. Ask your parents to help you check out athletic leagues in your town. Sometimes organizations like the Boys Club, Girls Club, or YMCA put together community teams for sports like skating, bowling, or horseback riding.

If you're into an art like karate or dance, you might have to pay for private lessons since most schools don't offer these activities. Also, if you're really into acting and you want to do more of it than your school offers, look for a community playhouse in your area. They may have a youth theater program or summer camp where you can get more experience in your craft.

Or maybe you're more interested in volunteering your time. One of the easiest places to volunteer at your age is a hospital or senior citizens' home, where you can bring folks flowers, refill water pitchers, and help out the nurses. (This is also a great way to get a little early experience if you're interested in a career in medicine!) You can also help at your town's soup kitchen—either by serving food or collecting food donations from people on your street. Or if you like animals, call your local humane society or ASPCA.

If you're interested in community service, ask your school guidance counselor if he or she knows of any organizations that are in need of volunteers. Also, community organizations like Boys Clubs and Girls Clubs often have volunteer programs. And finally, you should check out the Internet to find cool volunteer opportunities in your area. There are lots of Web sites that have info about volunteering, like www.idealist.org. You might also try the Web site of a specific organization, like the Salvation Army (www.salvationarmy.org) or Red Cross (www.redcross.org).

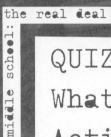

QUIZ:
What's the Best
Activity for You?

Answer true or false to the following questions:

true/false

1. I like being the center of attention.

true/false

2. I'd rather work on a project solo than as part of a group.

true/false

3. People say I'm kind of dramatic.

true/false

4. It embarrasses me when the teacher praises my work in front of the class.

true/false

5. I'd rather star in a play than write one.

true/false

6. If I don't have plans on a Friday night, I'd rather go for a bike ride by myself than call a friend and hang out.

true/false

7. If my school needed to raise money for a new library, I'd suggest a talent show over selling candy bars.

true/false

8. On Career Day, I'd steer clear of the local congressman who's looking for students to speak at a rally.

Scoring

- Award yourself two points for every true you circled on questions 1, 3, 5, and 7. Award yourself one point for each false you circled for these questions.

- Award yourself one point for every true you circled on questions 2, 4, 6, and 8. Award yourself two points for each false you circled for these questions.

If you scored 14 to 16 . . .

You love being center stage!

Consider these extracurricular activities: drama club, choir, student council, language clubs, sports like baseball, football, or tennis.

If you scored 11 to 13 . . .

You love being on the team!

Consider these extracurricular activities: student council, volunteering, sports like soccer or basketball.

If you scored 8 to 10 . . .

You love being behind the scenes!

Consider these extracurricular activities: student newspaper, yearbook, stage crew, sports like track and field.

But I'd Rather Be

making

some

money . . .

If you want to earn some extra cash, you might find yourself passing up extracurricular activities in favor of an after-school job. What kind of moneymaking opportunities are available for somebody your age?

Well, since you can't legally have a payroll job until you're 14, and even then you need a work permit until you're 18, and you can't drive until you're 16 (or 17 in some states), your options may be somewhat limited. But there are still a few simple ways to earn a little money without all the red tape:

Baby-sit
Dog-sit or cat-sit when people go on vacation
Offer a dog-walking service
Do yard work, like raking leaves or shoveling snow
Get a paper route (if you have a bike)

Try to get jobs through your neighbors or your parents' friends. Some people put up flyers in the grocery store to offer their services, but that's risky—you don't know the people who might be calling your house or hiring your services. We recommend that you get jobs through people you know instead. It's safer, and if you work hard, you'll get a lot of repeat business.

How to Get Tons of Business

Get the word out that you're a responsible worker by following these golden rules at all times.

Rule #1: Make sure your client has a reliable way of reaching you. Distributing handmade business cards is a good idea.

Rule #2: If you have to cancel, give your client plenty of notice. Never, ever leave somebody hanging without giving them the courtesy of a phone call.

Rule #3: Never use your work time for goofing around—especially if your client pays you by the hour.

Rule #4: Never abuse your client's home. Although most people don't mind if you make local phone calls or watch TV after their child is in bed, don't invite friends over or take your clients' belongings home.

Rule #5: Don't be afraid to ask questions. You aren't expected to know exactly how everything is done in another person's home, and your client would probably prefer that you ask instead of doing the job wrong.

Rule #6: If your client ever does something that makes you feel uncomfortable, tell your parents immediately. If you feel really uncomfortable, you can always quit.

As you can see, the possibilities for after-school activities are really almost endless. We hope you don't feel over-whelmed. The key is, all these activities are ways of learning more about life and the world. So whether you join a club, play a sport, volunteer, or mow lawns, do some-thing. Get involved. You'll have more fun— we guarantee it.

Now, on to what may be the scariest topic of all: school and your social life.

Chapter 4

friends, cliques, crushes,

and Other Social Stuff

iddle school seems to be the

time when the social scene really starts

to count. Maybe it's because everyone is

starting fresh instead of going back to

the same places and people they've

grown up with for years. Or maybe it's

because middle schoolers are almost

teenagers and are starting to go through

the huge physical and emotional changes that come with adolescence. Whatever the reason, you'll probably find that you're facing a much wider range of social issues now, from problems with friends, to negotiating cliques, to crushing, to being cool, to handling bullies. And then some! Read on for our words of wisdom.

friends

As we've already said, middle school is a time for big changes. This will almost definitely include changes in the way you deal with your friends and, often, in who your friends are. But though this adjustment may be hard at times, it's not necessarily a bad thing. You're growing and changing, and so are your friends.

By the way, we're not saying that you have to ditch all your old friends the moment you walk through the front doors of middle school. Not at all! Although we certainly think it's a good thing to make new friends, old friends can be a lifeline in this strange and, perhaps, stressful situation you're in. It can also be really comforting to discover that your friends are wrestling with many of the same issues as you are. It makes getting through the hard times a little less hard.

So how do you deal with friends, new and old? Read on for our best advice.

how can I tell if we're really really FRIENDS?

With all the new people you'll meet in middle school, how do you know which of them are true friends—people you can really trust and rely on?

Consider these pointers:

- You don't spill each other's secrets or gossip about each other.

- You don't compete or try to make each other jealous.

- You help each other when you're upset, sick, or having a bad day.

- You can be honest with each other.

what kind 4 • friend is that?

You're going to be meeting lots of different kinds of people, and chances are good that not every single one of them is going to turn out to be your soul mate. That's fine. We think it's more interesting to be friends with a wide variety of people. Here are some common personality types and suggestions for the best ways to negotiate a friendship with them.

The User

How to recognize one:

A friend like this might seem to really like you, always calling you up and inviting herself over for an unplanned pool party, or suggesting that you two get together and study, or wanting to get ready for a party together. But after a while you start to wonder if she really likes you—or if she's more interested in your in-ground pool, your homework (which she's always trying to copy), or your wardrobe (which she's always asking to borrow clothes from). You might also notice that when you need help, poof! She's suddenly gone.

How to deal with one:

Stick up for yourself. If you feel that a friend is taking advantage of you, don't let her push you around. For instance, if she sleeps over at your house one Saturday night and spends the whole time watching your big-screen satellite TV, then asks to sleep over again the next weekend, you might say, "Let's stay at your house this weekend." Give her a chance. Sometimes users aren't aware that they're being selfish. And who knows? If the two of you hang out and have a conversation rather than simply watching TV all night, you might actually discover some cool things about each other! If this doesn't work, next time she calls to invite herself over, you can tell her you already have plans.

The "Me"-aholic

How to recognize one:

Every conversation revolves around his problems and his life—he never asks what's going on with you. It seems like he's always leaning on you, but when you have something to get off your chest, he tends to zone out.

How to deal with one:

Although it shows that you're a great listener and easy to talk to, you shouldn't put up with being somebody's psychiatrist. When he starts to ask for advice, try turning the conversation to yourself by saying, "Let's talk about this first—I could use your help." If he hears you out and offers some advice or sympathy, this friendship is heading in the right direction. But if he can't figure out that friendship is a two-way street, maybe you need to take a step back.

The Control Freak

How to recognize one:

This type usually has a lot of friends—because she's bossy. She's always telling you what to do, what not to do, who's cool to hang out with, and so on. When you hang out together, the spotlight is always on her.

How to deal with one:

Declare your independence! Next time she says, "This is what we're doing, and these are the only people who can come," express your own opinion. If she wants to hang at the mall, but you'd rather go in-line skating, let her know. Then go ahead and do your thing—even if it means doing it alone. The control freak will learn that in order to be your friend, she'll have to let you make some of the decisions—and that's what a friendship is all about, anyway, right?

The Gossip

How to recognize one:

He's up on all the latest rumors—and that makes him popular since almost everybody likes to hear gossip. Also, he tends to ask you really personal questions, and he won't give up until he gets answers!

How to deal with one:

If you like gossip, a friend like this is a blast. But think hard before you spill any of your own secrets. Chances are, if you tell him something juicy, it will be all over school the next day.

The Backstabber

How to recognize one:

This is the person who'll steal your boyfriend or girlfriend or exclude you from a party. He or she wants to make you feel insecure because that makes him or her feel more important.

How to deal with one:

Your first impulse might be to get revenge—perhaps steal your backstabbing pal's crush or spread gossip. But take it from us, revenge rarely makes anyone feel better. Unfortunately, the only good way to deal with backstabbers is to make it impossible for them to hurt you—by putting some distance between yourself and them.

Best Friend FAQs

Q: Do I have to have a best friend—or can I have more than one best friend?

A: No to the first question and yes to the second. While it's important to have close friends, you don't have to have someone you call your "best" friend. You just need people you can lean on when the road gets bumpy. If you've got that, you're lucky. And as far as having more than one best friend, if that's the case, good for you! Just be careful about throwing around that term *best friend*. If you call someone your best friend, you're letting everybody else know they aren't as special to you, which can hurt.

Q: Can my best friend be of the opposite sex?

A: You wouldn't judge a best friend on the basis of religion or race, right? So why would you exclude half the human population from being your best friend? If you get support and understanding from a friend, that's all you need—it doesn't matter whether your pal is a girl or a guy. The only thing to watch out for is mixing up a best friend with a crush. (For more on that, see "Crushing," p. 102.)

Q: What do I do with my old best friend if I make a new one?

A: Strong friendships have to be flexible. Of course you can still hang out with your old best friend. It might not always be easy, but make the effort to stay close. After all, you two have a lot of history together. It's like that old saying: Make new friends, but keep the old. One is silver, and the other's gold!

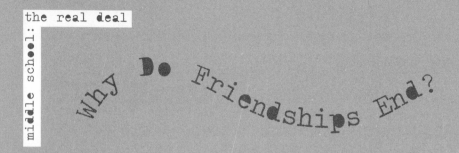

Why Do Friendships End?

As we mentioned above, now that you're in middle school, you might find that you just don't get along as well as you used to with the people who were your best friends just last year in elementary school. What's happening?

Well, it could be one of several things ...

1. People change. Sounds simple, but it's actually a pretty profound statement. As you start to mature, it's inevitable that your personality is going to change. Maybe you were shy in elementary school, but now you want to be more outgoing. This can cause a major shift in your friendships. If you become chatty and adventurous but your best friend is still in her shell (or the other way around), you might find yourself spending less time with her.

2. Interests change. Maybe you and your best friend were both obsessed with a particular video game, and you used to play it head-to-head every day after school. But now you've joined the school chorus and discovered that you want to be a singer. Or maybe your friend has joined the basketball team and has figured out that he likes being a jock. If you lose your common interests, you could lose the glue that kept the friendship alive.

3. You get competitive. If you start feeling like your friend has become better looking or more popular than you, you're probably going to get jealous. Who wouldn't? But competition can break up a friendship. Jealousy can cause friends to hurt each other—whether that means being overly critical or getting into fights over small disagreements.

4. One of you starts dating. If you and your best friend used to spend all your time together, but now she has a boyfriend, you might find that suddenly she's spending all her time either with him or talking about him. In that case, it's likely that you're going to feel left out—and maybe a bit resentful. A good way to compensate is by branching out and making new friends on your own. But don't be too hard on your old friend—love makes people do crazy things. And if her new relationship takes a dive, chances are she's going to turn to you for a shoulder to cry on. Try to be there for her.

CLIQUES:
WHAT ARE THEY,
AND why do people JOIN THEM?

Middle school is probably the place where you'll come face-to-face with cliques for the first time. What is a clique, anyway? Well, it's a group of people who hang out only with each other and refuse to let others join in. Cliques, like clubs, tend to form around people who have common interests or come from a common background. The problem with cliques is that they tell you who you can and can't be friends with. Saying other people can't join your club is a mean way to make yourself feel important.

The funny thing is, cliques can also cause major stress for the people in them. Instead of spending your time becoming friends with people who share your interests or exploring new stuff that interests you, you're restricted to a certain group. If the members of your clique see you becoming close with somebody they don't like, they might hassle you—or worse, kick you out of the clique.

So if they're so bad, why do people join cliques? The main reason is that it's an easy way to gain an instant group of friends and a sense of belonging. Also, the people in cliques are often the most popular kids in school. So if being friends with the coolest kids is important to you, you might end up in a clique.

Our two cents: Even if you choose to join a clique, you should strive to make or keep your own friends outside the group. Also, join activities and clubs because you're interested in them—not because your friends are there. True friends will stand by your side even when you do something uncool. You deserve friends who'll stick with you no matter what. Chances are, people in a clique won't stick around during the hard times.

CRUSHING

We're pretty sure that even back in elementary school, you had plenty of crushes. The symptoms? You thought about your crush all the time, every time you saw your crush your heart would beat a little faster, you got nervous around your crush, and so on. But you probably kept your feelings to yourself—or at least you didn't tell anyone besides your best friend.

But in middle school you'll notice that people are starting to be more open about their crushes. You'll probably get to know who in your class has a crush on whom. You'll probably even know some people who take it a step further and actually start dating. In fact, you might even start dating yourself! Yes, you!

Okay, now that you've had a second to get over the shock, read on for some tips on what to do when you're crushing like crazy.

How Do I Find Out if My Crush Crushes Back?

Well, there are several ways you could do this. Some strategies are riskier than others. You need to decide how comfortable you are about being bold.

The bold strategy: Approach your crush and flat-out tell him how you feel. This is something to try only if you have some reason to believe your crush actually might return the feeling. For example, if you've noticed your crush staring at you the last three or four times you checked him out—and you're sure it's not because you have ketchup on your face.

The slightly-less-bold-but-still-effective strategy: Strike up a conversation. Don't declare your love or anything; just ask your crush what she is up to, what she did that weekend, or if she gets as bored in math class as you do. If your crush never noticed you before, she will now—and that's the first step toward getting her to crush back. Besides, getting to know your crush will help you sort out whether your feelings for her are real or not.

The devious strategy: Have a friend check out the scene. Got a smooth friend who's good at being subtle? Have him or her talk to your crush. Maybe your detective pal can figure out whether your crush likes you back. Caution: There are a couple of ways this could backfire. One is that your friend could mess up and your crush could find out that you've been scoping out the situation. The other is that your smooth friend could end up getting interested in your crush, too.

The slow-and-steady strategy: Find ways to hang out in groups. If you learn that your crush is headed to the mall this weekend with friends, get your posse together and plan a rendezvous. Being in a group will make you more relaxed than you would be one-on-one—which may make it easier to strike up a casual conversation. But a drawback of this strategy is that if you're with a bunch of other people all the time, you may never get the chance to be one-on-one with your crush.

What to Do When Your Crush Isn't Crushing Back

It would be a perfect world if everybody you had a crush on liked you back. But if you're like most people, rejection is something you'll have to face every now and then.

If you've asked somebody out (or even just flirted with someone) and gotten the cold shoulder, it's natural to be embarrassed. But don't start thinking less of yourself. Your crush's reason for turning you down may have nothing to do with you. Maybe he isn't allowed to date yet but is too embarrassed to tell you. Or maybe he's scared—maybe the whole idea of going out with somebody makes your crush break into a cold sweat. Or maybe your crush is already crushing on somebody else, and there's no room in his brain to even consider you.

Whatever the reason, don't hang your head, and definitely don't feel like you have to avoid your crush. Try and act natural around him. Yes, easier said than done, we know. But you'll be proud of yourself for acting in such a mature way. And hey, you never know. Maybe your crush will reconsider when he sees how cool you are!

What Do Boyfriends and
Girlfriends Do?

Okay, so let's say you've actually connected with your crush and found out that the feeling is mutual. You've agreed to be a couple. So . . . what do you do now?

Lots of couples in middle school just hang out, talk on the phone, walk home from school together, and pass notes. Many of them never even kiss or hold hands! It doesn't mean it isn't a real relationship—it just means they're getting comfortable with the relationship in small steps. Taking your time is the smart thing to do!

But if you're blanking out on ways to pass your time together, here are a few ideas:

Go see a movie. Nothing could be finer than sharing some chills and thrills at the latest horror flick or laughing out loud together at a comedy.

Grab something to eat. We're not talking about a four-star restaurant here—just the local diner or hang-out spot.

Go shopping at the mall. Looking around in stores by yourself is fun. Looking around in stores with someone you like is even better.

Spend a day at an amusement park. What's not fun about going on lots of rides? Besides, the roller coaster is a great excuse to hold hands—and the Ferris wheel can be pretty romantic at sunset!

103

silly
love
moves

There are a few common sins that people commit when they're starting to date somebody. Read the words in quotes out loud and swear you'll stick by them.

1. "I won't ignore my friends." It's so easy to get wrapped up in a relationship and stop spending time with your friends—but we guarantee it will result in your friends having hurt feelings. Be sure that you divide your time equally between your boyfriend or girlfriend and your pals. If you spend Friday night with one, spend Saturday night with the other.

2. "I won't let schoolwork slide." You'd like to spend hours on the phone, chatting (or instant messaging on your computer) with the person you like. But you won't be able to do that if your parents ground you for getting bad grades! It's okay to talk, but know when it's time to say, "Gotta run." Besides, nothing is more attractive than a smart and responsible boyfriend or girlfriend.

3. "I'll still be my own person." Your friends are glad that you're happy—but they don't need to hear about every cute thing your significant other did or said. It can get really boring for them. Keep up with your schoolwork, extracurricular activities, and hobbies—and talk about that stuff as much as you talk about your relationship. This will also help to ease any jealous feelings your single friends may have over your relationship.

What Goes on at School Dances?

Dances are usually held in the cafeteria or gym on a Friday or Saturday night. The room will be decorated, and there'll probably be colored lights and maybe even a disco ball. A few teachers will be there as chaperons, but they pretty much keep to the background and watch as everybody cuts loose on the dance floor.

What will you dance to? A disc jockey (DJ) who's been chosen by the student council will play dance music. (If you're interested in getting into the planning of the dance, read about joining the student council in chapter three.) Usually you can even dedicate or request a song if you want to. The DJ will play mostly fast songs, but there may also be a few slow songs in there. These days girls ask guys to dance just as often as guys ask the girls, so if you have the nerve, go ahead and ask somebody—even if it's just a friend.

You've never danced before? Or you think you can't dance? That isn't an excuse to sit against the wall and be bored all night. The point of dancing is to let it all hang out and have fun. There's no such thing as right or wrong. If you're nervous, watch the way other kids move on the dance floor. Find a few whose style works for you—and follow their lead until you find a comfortable move of your own. And don't worry, chances are nobody's staring at you. Everybody feels self-conscious at a dance. They're so worried about their own moves that they won't actually pay much attention to your dancing skills—unless you're standing on the floor not moving at all!

the BREAKUP

Sometimes a relationship just doesn't work out. How it ends is up to you—it can be messy and hurtful, or it can end in friendship. If you're in a relationship that you no longer want to be in, it's your responsibility to talk with your boyfriend or girlfriend.

How do you know the relationship should end? Well, check out these common warning signs:

You no longer feel comfortable around the person.

You don't have fun when you're with him or her.

You'd much rather be spending time with your friends.

Now that you've gotten to know your boyfriend or girlfriend, you don't feel the same way about him or her anymore.

You have a heavy crush on somebody else.

If two or more of these warning signs are true for you, here's what to do. Talk to your boyfriend or girlfriend about your feelings. And we mean face-to-face. Don't write a note, don't send an e-mail, don't say it to an answering machine, and don't bring it up in the cafeteria when all your friends are around. This conversation should be private.

Try to explain, as gently as possible, that you think it's best if you stop dating each other, and apologize if you've hurt him or her. If he or she asks, you should offer some kind of explanation—whether it's, "I don't have enough time to spend on my schoolwork," or, "My feelings have changed, and I think of you more as a friend." These excuses may sound lame or overused to you, but maybe the reason they're used so often is because they're so often true.

What if someone breaks up with you? We won't lie—being dumped is much harder than dumping somebody. But if someone breaks up with you, you should try to act responsibly. Don't spread gossip about your ex, and don't ignore him or her when you see each other in gym. If you need some time to get over the hurt, take it. Just don't be mean. It won't make you feel better in the long run. One important thing to remember is, it's the other person's loss because you are cool and worthwhile. Lean on your friends during this rough stretch. After a little healing time, who knows? You may start getting butterflies in your stomach over somebody new.

Cool Style

While it's always important to be cool, middle school is often the place where being cool seems to matter more than anything else. We're going to let you in on a secret: Coolness is all about confidence. If you're comfortable with yourself and not afraid to show who you are, it's almost certain that other kids will think you're cool.

The Cool You

At this point you might be saying to yourself, "But how can I possibly feel confident? There's so much wrong with me!"

It may seem that way to you. But if you think about it, there are probably a lot of things you like about yourself, too. Make a list of the qualities you have that you love to show off. Then make a list of the qualities that you'd like to change. Check out this example:

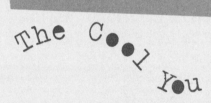

The Good
- bright smile
- tall
- great guitar player
- honor student

The Bad
- shy
- insanely curly hair
- horrible singing voice

If this list were yours, you could offer guitar lessons or tutor elementary school kids after school. And you could try out for the basketball team. How cool is that?

But what about the stuff on the "bad" list? Well, let's start with shy. Shy is an attitude, nothing more. And attitudes are not carved in stone. With some effort, you can change it. Start small—try smiling at one person you don't know but wish you did. You've got a killer smile, remember? And if a smile leads to a conversation, well, so much the better!

Next, your insanely curly hair. You may hate it, but chances are there are some straight-haired kids out there who just wish they had your problem. The secret is not to fight your hair. Forget about chemical straighteners or combing it flat. Accept that it is what it is and figure out what you can do to make it work for you. Talk to a stylist. A good one should be able to find a style that really flatters you—and shows off that mane!

As for your horrible singing voice . . . well, lots of famous musicians have voices that are not what you would think of as conventionally beautiful. The most famous example is Bob Dylan, a sixties folk-rock star who's still going strong today. Ask your mom or dad to dig out an old Dylan album for you. No one could possibly argue that his voice is pretty—but it didn't matter for him. Why? Because he had the right attitude.

See? The things on your "bad" list really aren't so bad after all. All you have to do is realize that "cool" is all about how you see yourself.

Clothes and Stuff

That said, we will admit that sometimes it's easier to feel cool and confident when you know your clothes and your stuff are just right. The problem is, keeping up with trends can get pretty expensive. Here are a few ideas on how you can stay on the cool track—without going into debt:

• Instead of splurging on every CD a certain band has ever made, ask to tape a friend's copy. You'll save big bucks, and you'll still be able to talk about the latest tunes with your friends.

• Be a smart shopper. Instead of going all out and buying an entire outfit, think small—buy a hat, a T-shirt, or a pair of shoes. You'll get major style points for knowing what's cool and still have cash left over.

- Dig through the racks at discount stores. Sometimes they'll sell a designer piece that somebody returned to a department store for half the price.

- Read magazines from the school library instead of buying them.

- Stock your wardrobe with Dockers and jeans, plain T-shirts and button-downs. The basics never go out of style, and you can wear the trendy stuff as accessories.

Why Does Cool Change So Quickly?

TV commercials. Magazine ads. Web sites. They're all competing for you to buy their products. You're bombarded with so many choices and options that it's hard to figure out what pants or makeup might be worth it and what's a waste of money.

Your age group is targeted by most large companies as the hottest group to sell to. Why? Because they know that being cool is more important to you guys than it is to almost anyone else. They know you're worrying about how you look, what you eat, what you listen to, and what you watch. And they're hoping to cash in on that! Clothing companies and video game companies spend all their time trying to invent the next trend and get kids like you to buy their product. Basically, cool changes quickly because there's so much stuff out there for you to choose from.

Think about that the next time you're watching a commercial for cargo pants and saying to yourself, "I've gotta have those!"

But I like being different

While some people like doing all the stuff that's popular with their peers—going shopping, in-line skating, checking out the latest horror flick—there are a few who prefer to stand apart and express themselves in different ways. Whether it's wearing business suits to school or listening to classical music, some kids aren't afraid to be a little different.

The pluses of being radical . . .

- You feel comfortable expressing yourself.
- You don't worry about what others think of you.
- You'll never blow a bunch of money on something just because it's in.

Bottom line: There should be a little bit of a radical in everybody—including you. If you enjoy something that isn't popular—whether it's swing dancing or collecting comic books—don't hide it. It could be the very thing that defines your own unique, personal style.

Why Do Bullies, Well, Bully?

Does a certain someone always have a sarcastic comment to make about your outfit? Or does some big kid threaten you to get you to hand over your lunch money? Maybe someone calls you names in the hall. It all falls under the category of bullying.

The first thing to do with a bully is to try to put yourself in his or her shoes. Think about why this person finds it so important to give you a hard time. Believe it or not, usually bullies are trying to make up for something that they think is wrong with them. Maybe the kid who's bullying you isn't a very good student. Or maybe he's upset because he didn't make the soccer team. Or maybe she thinks she's ugly or awkward. It's almost always the case that bullies intimidate others to feel better about themselves.

So how can you get a bully to back off? Your first strategy is to ignore him or her. Just walk away, and don't show any fear. Once the bully realizes that you won't react, he or she will probably get bored and move on.

Can't walk away? Okay, try to respond to a bully in a calm, rational way. Don't stoop to the bully's level. Don't hurl insults or get into a fight. Often that's just what a bully wants—an explosion. Also, fighting back will probably provoke the bully to more bullying behavior. It may be really hard, but you've got to try to keep your cool.

If you've tried keeping your cool or walking away and nothing seems to work, then don't hesitate to talk to a teacher or guidance counselor about a bully. You know what? That may actually be what the bully hopes you'll do, deep down. Lots of bullies are really looking for attention. So, hey, maybe you're actually doing someone a favor.

And that's what we have to say about the social scene in middle school. You'll probably come across some other issues as time goes by, but this should give you a reasonable overview of what to expect.

That takes care of school. But what about your home life? It may sound crazy, but sometimes parents have a harder time getting used to middle school than their kids do. Keep reading for the scoop. . . .

Chapter 5

Why Are My Parents still treating me LIKE A BABY?

Once you enter middle school, the days of Mom bringing cupcakes to class are officially over—but even though she knows this, she still might have a hard time letting you go. She's used to you being her baby, and in the next few years that's the last thing that you'll want to be.

As you grow into young adulthood, you'll also develop an adult way of thinking—and that means you'll probably want to spend a lot less time with your parents. But you can't just flick an I-need-my-privacy switch. You'll almost certainly have to survive some growing pains before you and your parents settle into a relationship you're both comfortable with. This chapter will explore many of the issues you'll probably face with your mom and dad. Use these tools to help make your family ride smoother.

why won't my PARENTS let go?

Some common complaints middle schoolers have about their parents are:

- "They still treat me like a baby!"

- "They're so embarrassing. They always want to talk to my friends and me."

- "They're always asking me a million questions. Why can't I have any privacy?"

- "With all these rules, it's like they don't trust me at all."

What's up? Have your parents suddenly lost their minds?
Not quite. The truth is a little more complicated.

Try to imagine this: You wake up one morning, and your dad
is ... different. Instead of being his usual chatty self, he's quiet and
wants to be left alone. You used to watch TV together on week-
nights, but now he goes out after work and doesn't come home
until 10 P.M.—and then he just goes straight to bed. He won't tell
you what he's up to, and he gets mad if you ask too many questions.

If this happened, wouldn't you feel hurt? Think about it.
Because this is a lot like what your parents are going to go
through with you.

When you were in elementary school, you probably told
your parents everything—what you were studying, what you did
with your friends that day, what was bugging you if you were in a
bad mood. But a natural part of growing up is leaning more on
your friends than on your parents for support. So don't be surprised if you find yourself pouring out your heart to your friends
and keeping your parents in the dark.

To your mom and dad, the change in your behavior will probably cause some confusion and anxiety. Especially your new independence. If your parents are suddenly laying down a million
rules, this is probably why. It's not that they don't trust you—it's
just that they're worried about you.

It might take them a while to learn how to interact with this
new adult in their house. But try to be patient with them. Give
them some time to get used to the new you. After all, they're
only bugging you because they love you.

How Can I GET SOME PRIVACY?

One of the major face-offs you'll probably have with your parents will involve your need to hang out in your room . . . alone. Maybe your mom is used to cleaning out your school bag, or it's your dad's job to gather up your dirty clothes for the laundry. Suddenly you might find yourself not wanting them to go through your stuff. It feels like they're violating your privacy.

So how do you avoid World War III in your bedroom? Well, why not start by taking responsibility for all chores that involve your room? Here are some changes you can make that will help you avoid parental meltdowns:

- Keep your room relatively clean. We're not saying you have to make your bed army style every morning. But don't keep greasy food containers in your room. Try to put the bulk of your stuff away when you're not using it. Toss your dirty clothes into a hamper rather than just piling them in the middle of your floor. This will keep your parents from invading to organize your personal stuff.

- Do your own laundry. That way your parents won't have to dig through your pockets—where they might find notes that you'd rather keep private.

- Stash your school bag in your bedroom instead of in the family area. This will end the temptation of nosy siblings or parents to peek at your stuff.

- When you borrow something from Mom or Dad, return it—otherwise they may have to search your room to find their shirt or perfume.

- Follow the house rules. If you want to burn candles in your room but your mom is worried about fires, respect that. Don't sneak and light a candle when she's not home. Chances are she'll find out—and then she'll feel she can't trust you.

What should you do if you discover that your privacy has been violated? First, resist the urge to scream. Come on, they're still your parents—and it's their house, too.

Once you're breathing normally again, talk to your parents. You need to let them know, calmly and respectfully, that you would appreciate it if your room were off-limits. Ask them—nicely—to come to you if there's something they need or if there's a problem. Be mature and responsible and they'll be much more likely to listen to you.

And that's the key, really. If your parents come to you with a problem about your room, you can't say, "It's my room, and I like it that way." To keep moms and dads out of your space, you have to follow their rules. Learn that valuable lesson and you'll have all the privacy you need.

Which leads us to the bigger issue: trust.

How do I gain my Parents' trust?

Picture this: You invite your new math study partner over for a cram session the day before a big test. Study partner happens to be a pretty cute specimen of the opposite sex. As you lead him/her up to your room, your mom pops out from nowhere and introduces herself. Then, as you and your study partner head for the stairs, she pulls you aside and mutters, "Leave your bedroom door open while you study, please."

What is up with that? Now that you're in middle school, your parents suddenly seem to have gotten a new—and much bigger—book of rules than the one you used to go by. It may seem sometimes like your mom and dad are trying to stop you from doing anything more controversial than trying a different breakfast cereal. But don't get too freaked out. If they're suddenly being overprotective, it's because it's their way of coping with the changes you're going through. Follow these handy steps and you too can turn your overprotective folks into cool, laid-back parents.

Step 1:

Show 'em you're responsible. If it were up to your parents, they'd probably keep you locked in the house 24/7. It's not that they want you around that much—it's just that they worry about you. To them the world's one big, scary place that's just waiting to gobble you up. In order to gain more freedom, you need to show your parents that you're responsible.

How? Keep them informed. Let Mom and Dad meet your friends—it helps when they know who you're hanging out with and where you're going. Also, you'd be surprised how far a phone call home can go. If you're running late or your plans change, let your parents know. It only takes a minute to ease their minds—and make yourself look pretty responsible at the same time.

Step 2:

Follow the rules. What pushes your parents over the edge? When you forget to empty the lint trap in the dryer? Leave dirty dishes in the sink? Whatever it is, cross it off your to-do list. In fact, think of the top-five things that drive them nuts and eliminate all five behaviors from your life.

Why bother? Because if you try harder to eliminate the top-five pet peeves, your parents will probably cut you a little more slack when you mess up in some other way. They may think, "Well, Joe accidentally broke the CD player when he was playing carpet hockey in the living room—but on the other hand, he hasn't left his breakfast dishes in the sink for a week. He's trying. Maybe I shouldn't ground him for life."

Step 3:

Choose your battles wisely. Sometimes fighting with your parents is worth the effort—for example, if they read your journal or give away your favorite jacket to your younger cousin. In cases like this it's important for you to stand up and tell your parents that they've invaded your privacy.

But sometimes fighting with your parents isn't worth the effort. Sometimes you might pick fights with your mom or dad over stupid or trivial things just because you're in a bad mood. The thing is, the more you fight with your parents, the less inclined they'll be to actually listen to you. So if you blow up at them every time they do anything even slightly annoying, they'll just tune you out in the future, even if that time you're fighting about something that's really important to you.

Next time you feel a bad mood coming on, spend a moment alone. It'll save you from going off on someone who doesn't deserve it and give your real, legitimate arguments more power.

Step 4:

When you get caught, face the music. Come on—when you break the rules, you almost always know you're doing it. Whether it's as little as snacking before dinnertime or as big as sneaking out after curfew, you probably choose to cut loose and ignore the rules every now and then. And every once in a while, you will get caught.

If you want to build a stronger relationship with your parents, the first thing you need to do when you get busted is to admit you were wrong. And be specific about it. "I know I'm not supposed to swing from the chandelier because it's dangerous. I'm sorry, and I won't do it again." Then accept your punishment without whining or crying.

Step 5:

Learn the art of getting rules changed. Your parents probably have a few rules that you think are pretty silly or downright unfair. Maybe it's no phone calls after 9 P.M. or only one hour of TV each day.

How can you get them to change their ways? Here's a hint: Breaking the rules won't help.

As a matter of fact, if you want to get a rule changed, you must first prove that you can stick to it. So if you're trying to get your weekend curfew changed from 9 P.M. to 10 P.M., you need to be sure you're home by 8:59 every night for at least a month before you can even think about asking.

Why go through the hassle? Think about this: If the last five times your friend borrowed a CD from you, it came back scratched, would you lend him or her your new CD Walkman? No way. But if you have a friend who always returns your CDs quickly and in perfect condition and this friend asks to borrow your new Walkman, you'll probably say, "Sure!"

Apply the same logic to your parents. Again, it's all about building trust. You won't get all the adult privileges you're looking for until you prove to your parents that you deserve those privileges. Start proving yourself trustworthy and reliable today, and you'll be there in no time.

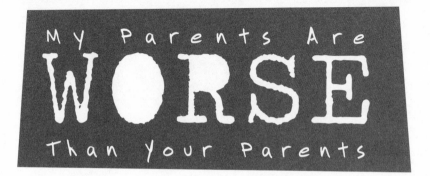

My Parents Are **WORSE** Than Your Parents

Are your parents really that bad? We didn't think so. But check out the list below to discover the different parental types and the best ways of handling each.

The type:

You're just a kid

The signs:

They don't take your opinions seriously, and they don't respect your right to privacy.

The real problem:

They don't want to acknowledge that you're growing up. (Note: This is different from the you're-my-baby parents, who just don't realize what's going on.)

How to get along:

You have to understand that your parents are acting this way basically out of fear of change. Make it easier for them by showing them that change isn't necessarily a bad thing. Now that you're older, you're actually less of a handful, not more. In practical terms it helps to make your parents aware of your achievements—whether we're talking about making the honor roll or finishing your chores early. Keep showing them how responsible and mature you are, and they'll start to relax.

The type:
You're my baby

The signs:
They're always fussing over your clothes, hugging you, telling you how special you are, and urging you to eat your broccoli.

The real problem:
Well, it's embarrassing—especially in front of other people. But it also suggests that they don't realize how quickly you're growing up.

How to get along:
When you're alone, express your concerns to your parents when they treat you like a baby. Ask them to save nicknames and other babyish treatment for home. But be sure not to say it in a harsh or disrespectful way, or you'll hurt their feelings.

The type:
You're my best friend

The signs:
They're up on all the gossip with your friends, and they may even wear the same style clothes as you.

The real problem:
You may feel like they're crossing over into your world. After all, your friends are your friends—and it's annoying to have your parents horn in.

How to get along:
It's fine to approach them for help when you have a fight with a friend—but it's better to leave them out of the loop when it comes to your friends' gossip. Find a nice way to tell them you'd rather keep your social life a little more separate. It's up to you to draw the line here since your parents won't.

EMBARRASS ME

Moms and dads have this natural gift—they know how to embarrass you like no one else on the planet. But it's not as if they do it on purpose. Here's how you can handle some of the most common cringe-worthy family situations.

Humiliation Factor

* SOMETHING'S STUCK BETWEEN YOUR FRONT TEETH . . .

** . . . WHILE YOU'RE TALKING TO YOUR CRUSH . . .

*** . . . AND THEN YOU REALIZE THAT YOUR BUTTON-FLY IS WIDE OPEN.

Scene: The Family Outing
Humiliation Factor: **

You're out to dinner with your family when you notice that the captain of your soccer team is at the next table. Cap comes over to say hello—and your mom picks that exact moment to reach over and cut up your chicken for you.

Avoid the embarrassment by: going over to the friend's table to talk for a minute instead of having him or her come to yours.

Scene: The Date
Humiliation Factor: ***

Your parents have been dreaming of your first date for as long as you have. When your date arrives, they sit him or her down in the living room and chat for a few minutes. You stand up to get your date a soda. But when you come back, your eyes widen with horror as you see that they've whipped out the baby pictures. Yes, the ones where you're naked.

Avoid the embarrassment by: timing your date activity (movie, outing with friends, whatever) so that there's only enough time for a very quick meet-and-greet session with your parents before you have to leave.

Scene: When They Try to Be Hip
Humiliation Factor: **

When it's your dad's turn to drive the carpool, he greets everybody with a, "Yo, homeboy!" Or your mom starts asking your girlfriends who their favorite Backstreet Boy is and saying, "I think the blond one is so cute!"

Avoid the embarrassment by: just grinning and bearing it. Hey, at least your parents are trying. What makes the situation really embarrassing is if you go off on your parents and call them on it. Instead, laugh a little! Chances are your friends will think your parents are cute.

Scene: Clothes Shopping
Humiliation Factor: *

Way back when, your parents used to pick out all your clothes for you. Now when you step out of the dressing room to show her the outfit you picked, your mom tests the waistband of your jeans. Then she makes you spin around again . . . and again . . . then loudly announces, "They're too tight! How about these cute slacks?"

Avoid the embarrassment by: calling Mom into the dressing room to check out the clothes instead of doing a mini–modeling show for the entire store. At least nobody will see you turn magenta while your mom tries to give you a nerd makeover.

The bottom line here is that you

need to keep in mind that your parents are

going through growing pains just the way

you are. So try to cut them a little slack—

without letting them keep you in diapers

forever.

conclusion

ow that you've read this book, doesn't middle school seem a lot less scary than it did before? From classes to friendships to heart-racing crushes, there are lots of new rules—but you know all about them now, so you'll blend in with the more experienced middle schoolers when September rolls around.

Just one last thing: Try this quiz to find out whether you slept through any of the great material in this book!

QUIZ:
Are You
Ready to Rule at
Middle School?

1. You don't like the fact that the choir performs only two concerts a year, so you:

a) complain to your friends about how lame the school is.

b) write a note to the choir director, asking him to do something about it.

c) ask the choir director if you can organize a group to sing the national anthem at football games.

2. Your history report on the French Revolution is due in two days, and so far all your group-project mates have done is goof off. You:

a) join in. You don't want to look like a smarty-pants.

b) finish your part of the project and make sure the teacher knows that you did everything you could.

c) tell everybody about your idea for bringing in French bread and Brie for extra credit, then help them come up with cool ideas.

3. Mom got a great new job, which is cool—except that now you have to cook dinner two nights a week while she works late. And that means missing two soccer practices. How do you deal? You:

a) quit the team. There's no way you can keep up if you can't make it to every practice.

b) tell Mom you're sorry, but you have to go to practice—you'll just have to eat pizza on nights that she works late.

c) look on-line to find some easy recipes for dinners you can freeze. That way you can prepare them on Sunday and just nuke 'em later that week.

4. A girl in your school's popular clique is having a pool party this weekend—and you're invited! You are so psyched. The problem is, you already had plans to hang with your best friend that day—and your best friend is not invited. You:

a) call your best friend up on Saturday morning and pretend you're sick in bed. Then you sneak off to the party and hope no one happens to mention it in front of your best friend next week in school.

b) tell your best friend about the party and ask if you two can hang out on Sunday instead.

c) ask the party's host if it's all right for you to bring a friend. If she says no (or wants to know who your friend is before she makes up her mind), you tell her that it's really nice of her to invite you, but you already have other plans that day. Maybe some other time. Then you and your best friend make your own party.

5. Oh, man—it looks like you're going to be spending another long Thanksgiving weekend at your aunt's house. Last year it was so boring, you fell asleep in the candied yams. You want it to be different this year, so you:

a) tell your parents there's absolutely no way you're going to your aunt's again this year. You're old enough to stay home alone.

b) beg them to let you bring a friend along so at least you won't be bored and lonely.

c) bust out the Jenga game after dinner and make the dull night a little more lively.

Scoring

Find the letter you selected most in the questions above, then read your answer section below.

If you chose mostly A's . . .
Giving Up

Well, when the going gets tough, you find a good hiding spot. Why are you so quick to slack off? Are you afraid you won't be able to reach your goals if you set them too high? Everything in life worth having takes work. And if you keep dodging it, you won't get very far. Start middle school right, and make a vow to quit complaining and jump into action when you see a problem.

If you chose mostly B's . . .
Getting There

You've got the right attitude. You don't hide from responsibilities, and you know how to think creatively—and that helps you be successful. But sometimes you fall back on the I'm-just-a-kid excuse a little too often. You're well on the way—just be sure to go that extra step to help out when you see someone in need.

If you chose mostly C's . . .
Going All the Way

How did you get to be such a superstar? You know what you want, and you know how to get it. That means erasing any trace of laziness and holding yourself to your responsibilities . . . even when all you want to do is take a nap! Teachers, friends, and even your family appreciate your reliability, and they respect you for being so mature. Friends and siblings should pick your brain to find out how they can hitch a ride on the Maturity Express.

Okay, now you're really set. If you aced the quiz, excellent. If you didn't, you know what you have to work on. By the time you show up for your first day of middle school, you are going to be so ready, you'll blow everyone else away.

And just wait—before you know it, you'll be one of those cool, laid-back older kids leaning against the lockers between classes. Then the kids a grade younger than you will be reading this book to find out how to be just like you.